We Play Sports

by Steve Jones

W9-BRY-508

Is it fun to play tennis?

net

Yes! I can hit a ball over the net!

Is it fun to play soccer, too?

Yes! I can kick a ball.

Is it fun to play golf, too?

grass

Yes! I can hit a ball over the grass!

Comprehension Check

Retell

Complete the Sequence Chart with your class. Then retell what you learned.

First
↓
Next
↓
Last

Think and Compare

1. What sport did you read about first? What sport did you read about next?

2. Which sport do you like best?

3. What sports have teams?